In This Moment of Freedom

Poetic Reflection Volume 1

by

Natalie Merritt-Broderick

IN THIS MOMENT OF FREEDOM
Poetic Reflection Volume 1
by Natalie Merritt-Broderick

Canadian Intellectual Property Office | An Agency of Industry Canada
Registration No.: 1148722 © 2018

Disclaimer
This book contains the thoughts, ideas and opinions of its author. The intention
of this book is to provide information, reflection and motivation to readers on
the subjects addressed. It is shared and sold with the understanding that the
author is not engaged to render any type of psychological, medical, legal or
any other kind of personal or professional advice. No warranties or guarantees
are expressed or implied by the author's choice to include any of the content
in this volume. The reader should always consult his or her medical, health or
other professional and accredited health provider before adopting any of the
suggestions in this book or drawing any ideas, inferences or practices from this
book. The author shall not be liable for any physical, psychological, emotional,
financial or commercial damages, including, but not limited to, special,
incidental, consequential or other damages. The reader is responsible for their
own choices, actions and results.

1st Edition, 1st printing 2018

Cover design by Steve Walters at Carolyn Flower International:
www.carolynflower.com
Interior design by Steve Walters
Author headshots by Emily Beatty Imagery: emilybeattyblog.com
Cover and interior photography by Natalie Merritt-Broderick

ISBN-13: 978-1985231849 (CreateSpace-Assigned)
ISBN-10: 1985231840

Introduction

The art of writing has always come easily for me. I am continually inspired by my ability to take ideas and swirl them into whatever creative artwork they need to be. As much as I love to write and get my thoughts on paper, I have never truly trusted enough in my talent to publish a book, even though I knew it was meant to be.

Many have said every journey begins with one step; this book has been a combination of many. Our lives were never meant to be complicated and we have all been brought into existence to learn and share our gifts with others. This is one of my gifts.

I have had many who have cherished my writing but as I have learned, no matter how many cherish my writing, I must cherish it first and foremost in order to make it a reality. Perhaps through my own journey, others will be inspired to look at their gifts and share them with the world.

The ability to inspire even one person, will bring a smile to my face. Never let anyone take your dreams away or tell you that you aren't good enough, because we are all valuable. Fly Be Free my friends and when you land, know the journey has been worth every soaring moment.

Contents

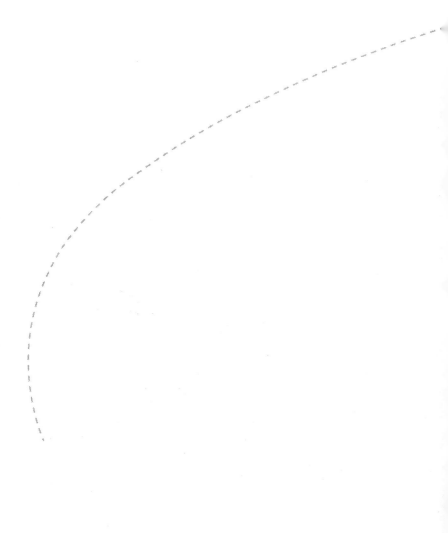

Abstracts

*It has never been my expectation
that everyone would understand
my thoughts.*

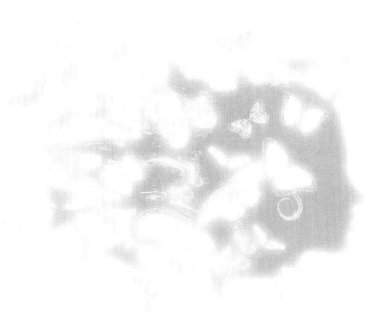

Abstracts

Characteristics of an object, colours in a spectrum.

Shapes in different dimensions.

Words, embellished and lengthy.

Understanding, tolerant and confused.

Feelings, drawn and examined.

Sight, pre-defined and indifferent.

Temperature, difficult and demanding.

Centuries, reminiscent and painful.

Family, intolerable and wise.

Friendship, aloof and unbiased.

Darkness, emptiness and comfort.

Books, in-depth and unreal.

People, fictitious and harmful.

The world is all these things; however, to each,
the picture reflects differently.

What Does this Mean?

It rains, it snows, the sun shines, the fog blinds.

What does this mean?

The wind howls, the sun blazes, the snow chills.

What does this mean?

The earth rotates, birds fly, children play.

What does this mean?

Television informs, radios advertise, tapes entertain.

What does this mean?

People are happy, people are sad, people are frustrated.

What does this mean?

Cars speed, trains kill, airplanes transport.

What does this mean?

In the grand scheme of things,
what does it matter in a world of differing opinions?

No Beginning, No End, No Meaning

Ice floats in many directions,
like trees blowing in an unruly hurricane.

Steps leading to nowhere and where is nowhere?

My isolation is futile for regardless of what I do,
someone will find me.

It may take time, but…

The clock of time will always find me for it has no end.

My freedom will be acknowledged by my own perseverance.

The boulder is as strong as I am weak.

He who knows everything knows absolutely nothing!

Shower Dreams

You contemplate your life in the shower as hot,
soothing water cascades down your body.

Running your hands through your hair, you
attempt with fragrant shampoo to wash away
all that bothers you, as if your world would
magically disappear down the drain with the
suds of shampoo, leaving the hot soothing water
to replace all that was wrong.

Your shower ends, then reality hits as
the curtain is drawn and your skin feels
the first, cold rush of factual air.

You shiver knowing the only thing that
has changed, is that you are now cleaner
than when you stepped into the shower
in the first place.

Mother's Wrath

We are but simple folk, attempting to
lead a life bereft of hardships.

If we are lucky and pay attention to our
surroundings, then anything is possible.

There are events; however, for which we
have no control; they are left in the hands
of another whose destruction or beauty
can change within a moment.

No matter the season or the reason, her mood
can disintegrate before our very eyes.

She is weapon of mass destruction
through means of drought, storms,
fires, tornadoes and flooding.

When truly vengeful to destroy, she may
combine many elements at one time.

Through it all she shows no mercy
for her destruction and is never
biased against just one.

Beauty

For you see, the sky is not always
clear and bright in my world,

Abandonment

A rustic building once a place of grandeur now
stands in disrepair as vines creep up its stone walls
and weeds now flank it from all sides.

The grass no longer emerald green or trimmed.

A home long forgotten, the laughter and
heartache of those who once inhabited it are
now distant memories.

Windows which once viewed the world are now
blinded with plywood sheets.

Trees once strong and tall are no longer protectors
from nature's wrath, their own gnarled and weak
limbs have fallen prey to time and must now care for
themselves instead of the house they once shielded.

Empty rooms fall prey to vagrant creatures.

The condemned building, offering warmth and
protection, is now their castle.

To the outside world it is nothing more
than a distant memory.

One onlooker feels its pain, as a reminder
of their own emptiness.

A fence has been built to hide its ugliness; yet,
IT is the real beauty.

The observer realizes its beauty even though
they have been blinded to their own, due to the
misguided words they have allowed to inhabit them.

Sun

Your silence is intoxicating.

Your beauty surpasses anything
I have seen in a very long time.

I imagine the freedom you have.

Each ending day you bring us to darkness by
slowly slipping lower into the west.

Each new day you bring us a life
full of wonder and surprise.

I have captured your beauty
as you have risen and fallen.

You grace my countryside with a peacefulness
unparalleled to anything I have felt within.

I will endeavour to enjoy your beauty the
rest of my life and when my eyes close for
the very last time, may it be on the wings of
a sunrise or sunset.

Flower Power

At the height of your existence, you are a symbol of infinite grace.

Through your many forms, you are likely to portray a multitude of characters.

Your fragrance resonates a sweetness and when blended with other subtle scents can send the most delicate of noses aflutter.

Your silky smooth petals caress even the roughest human hand.

Your beauty is displayed in infinite colour combinations and although you are not appreciated by all, you are appreciated by more than less.

Both butterfly and hummingbird once intertwined amongst your petals, create a spectacle of beauty that could only be created at the hand of nature's paint brush.

May we all find a way to embrace your magnificence, for to do any less would be a sin.

Sadness

I once ran from this place.

When I left, my heart and soul were dead.

My memories were anything but happy.

I felt no love in this place, only anger and
destruction.

When I stopped running it was because I had
found a place filled with love.

A place with caring people, who helped me see
beyond the darkness.

With the fear gone and knowledge of my own,
self-worth evident, I returned.

Now, instead of fear and hopelessness, I only
feel sadness for those years of long ago when
happiness should have been mine.

Flowers

Standing tall and fragrant in the summertime.

Giving way to the colder days of fall.

Buried far beneath the snow in the wintertime.

Then magically bursting forth during the rainy days of spring.

How beautiful is their progression, like that of us mere mortals going through our own profound stages of life.

Beauty

Beauty can be defined in many ways through
the hearts knowing.

Beauty could be defined by placing
no boundaries.

Beauty could be defined simply
through knowing.

Beauty could be defined by knowing we are all
unique and special.

Beauty could be defined by the abundant source
of strength we all possess, and drawn upon
whenever needed.

Beauty lives within, around us, and is
ultimately infinite.

These sentences define beauty for me.

They encourage me on the worst of days to
realize, I am beauty and that it surrounds me
even on those days when it is not clearly visible.

If you are unable to see or believe in beauty, close
your eyes and let your imagination lead the way.

And when the vision is clear and vivid in your
mind, store it in your heart and bring it forth on
those days when you doubt.

Destination

and that is okay with me.

Mirror Images

Through its silent presence, a mirror reflects so much to a person, be it sorrow or joy.

You are my mirror, my window to my soul.

Through your eyes, I see all that I can, need and want to be.

May I never lose you, my mirror, or the love you feel for me, for you bring me love and comfort through your somewhat jagged edges.

Understanding

I need to express my feelings but am wrestling with the words.

My inner voice condemns me to write, as my outside voice is unable to speak and in this situation my message must be to the point.

Till now my road in life has been obstructed by boulders and fallen trees. My attempts to clear the way have proved challenging and taken time, but due to my determination, I am here with you now.

Not all my cuts and bruises have healed and my faith is still fragile in many ways.

My feelings for you are strong and this is what scares me the most.

As feelings and memories from the past flood my imagination, my trust for your wavers. But you must realize, it is not you that I doubt - it is my ability to believe you would love me so deeply.

In time, self-doubt and fear will give way.

I hope you will accept my words and actions, as limited as they are, that the love we share together IS more powerful than my fears will ever be.

Imperfect is Perfect

I may not be able to stop all the bad habits.

I may not always be able to say the sweetest of words, and I may falter when I shouldn't.

I was not made perfect and of this I am glad, for I would have nothing in common with anyone else if I were.

Challenge

I walked down a roadway with tall stone walls
on either side.

I came to a hole in one of the walls.

I should have crawled through but
Fear stopped me.

Had I challenged Fear, I would have crawled
through the wall and been rewarded ten times
over for simply trusting in something greater
than Fear.

Never let Fear control your choices, for they are
not Fear's to make.

Standing Tall

A great pine stands in the backyard, its roots firmly planted deep in the ground.

The earth's nutrients help the tree grow tall and strong as its branches reach in varying directions.

Needles soft to the touch when stroked away from the tree become daggers when forced in the opposite direction.

Its branches give way to the wind, rain and even the heavy, wet snow of wintertime.

And yet, for all it suffers, it somehow manages to stay strong and does not let what Mother Nature tosses its way, defeat it.

One day, I will be that tree!

When Tomorrow Comes

I won't be judged for being imperfect.

I won't be criticized for not having done the same thing as you.

I won't be seen as needing 'constant' improvement.

I will be seen as a caring person, who tries to do the right thing most of the time.

For the rest of the time, I plan on being accepted for who I am, not for who you want me to be.

Your Journey into the Sunrise

I watch from a distance as you
head out the drive.

You reach the end, you stop.

I see you look left, look right and
then straight ahead.

I cross my arms and shift my weight and wonder
which way you will choose.

Like you, my own journey through life has
caught me off guard.

But no matter which way you go, no challenge
can be pre-ordained.

I watch for a while longer, then notice
you start to move, I can only surmise you
have made a choice.

Your destination should not matter to me as
I am not along for the ride.

I can only hope, as you turn out the drive
that you will eventually end up where you are
destined to be.

The Cycle of Life

We start out as a vision in someone's mind.

We are born and then morph into young children, who become teenagers, then adults.

Through each stage of our lives we experience new challenges, some good and some bad.

No matter your challenge or predicament, we need to embrace all that our lives have to offer, for do-overs are not guaranteed.

Freedom

You stand in a field surrounded by nothing,
yet in my mind, I see you lost in a maze of corn.
Your only visuals are the stalks and
the sky above.

I can see a pathway out but I know it is
not so clear to you.

Your motives may be honourable but are they
worth the sacrifices you feel you owe?

I have attempted to lead you into the open
where your viewpoint will be clearer.

Yet each time I turn around,
I have lost you once again.

As the moments become years, I know I must
leave you be, for it isn't up to me to get you out.

As I sit on the outer perimeter, I can only assume
we are at a crossroads, so I will continue on my
way and leave you to continue on yours.

If you ever wish my help, let me know and
I will gladly lend a hand in helping you
find your way out.

Pedestal

Have you ever looked around and realized,
you do not stand beside your comrades,
instead you tower over them?

If you have not noticed what is obvious, may I
suggest you look down and see how far above
them you have placed yourself.

By all means, feel free to embrace your
individuality but be wary of your
feelings of supremacy.

Feel blessed by what you have, but never allow it
to deflate the power of another.

Beware of the tight rope that you walk upon, for
if you fall, the drop will be considerable.

It may be wise for you to know the dangers of
being so high before it's too late, because when
you fall, there may be no one there to save you.

Destiny

When I look at you I see strength, but I wonder
how deep it goes.

Time has transported us further than I had ever
thought possible.

You have spent many years focused on me and
what I'm all about.

Trying to determine my complexity, am I
complicated or simple.

The trust between us is non-negotiable and how
you measure that is beyond my grasp.

Where trust is your concern, love is mine.

I am unable to describe the joy I feel and yet
I know it exists, especially when you hold me
close.

You question my love; but I need you to have
faith, for I treasure you as a friend, partner and
lover.

Where you go with our relationship, I cannot
foretell, nor do I want to try.

What I need you to realize is that I love you,
plain and simple.

Your strength, your weaknesses,
and all that you embody.

Destiny (continued)

With anticipation, I await the day when you feel
the same for me.

Or perhaps you already do?

I do not seek the world, for it isn't mine to own.

It's the feelings within your heart that most
concerns me now.

If I did not care, I would not ask.

But, you see, it is not just your future in the
balance, it is mine as well.

In This Moment of Freedom

Dream

My love is writing, and no matter what I write,
I don't need your approval.

The Wish

You always want what you can't have and
when the decision truly isn't yours,
you want it even more.

Perhaps because the dreams of others were
coming true, you were what I thought I wanted
but the words echoed to me by another,
indicated this was not the case.

Time ticked by and one day through a force
greater than I, my wish of being childless,
forever, came true.

I agonized over the unfairness because the choice
had never been mine to make.

As I watched those closest to me be given their
precious gift, all I could do was look on.

I was angry and hurt but for all
the wrong reasons.

As I look back now and deep into my heart,
I got my wish, just not the way I wanted it.

Follow the Leader

For each word I've spoken,
I've thought hundreds more.

Tonight, I have pen and paper in my hand.

I think to myself, 'no more TV for me,
close up house and write'.

As I enter the bedroom, words escape me and I
think, 'why bother'?

My focus is now gone.

I climb into bed and take note
of my beautiful dog.

She snores, as her eyes quietly
roll back into her head.

I take her lead, lay back on the mattress,
turn of the light and let my eyes roll back
into my head as well.

Thank you, God, for making my dog so smart.

Let the Future be Now

Let the day come when getting up isn't an issue.

Let the day come when all you have to worry about is being creative.

You search the deepest recesses of your mind and before you can catch your breath, the words begin to flow like a babbling brook.

And as the words continue to flow, you find the ink from your pen and the speed with which your hand writes are unable to keep up.

The once blank page is becoming alive with all your vivid thoughts, happy or sad, it does not matter.

For nothing is pure and simple.

And all you care about in this moment and time are the precious words and thoughts which one day will grant you the freedom you once only dreamed about.

A freedom that has always been yours for the taking, while your faith quietly denied it.

Solitude

If I could go to my most favourite place,
where would it be?

It would be a place that brought me
great inspiration.

It would calm me as my imagination ran wild.

It would be a place of enlightenment, where
I would hear all of nature's beauty in the
background and the unwanted noise of the
city would be miles away.

The early morning temperatures
would awaken my senses.

The afternoon sun would warm me, while the
evening sunset would allow me to end my day.

While others might wither from such solitude,
I willingly embrace its beauty.

Palace Life

A vast array of cultures, assemble late at night,
all churned into one.

The attitudes fluctuate,
dependent on the alcohol consumed.

Like characters in a novel,
their personalities vary.

Voices carry far and wide,
for most there are no boundaries.

Some become invincible, others fall prey to the
effects of the clear and not so clear liquids,
and still others change personalities altogether,
like that of Jekyll and Hyde.

Some retreat before the early light of dawn,
others only when the sun has
fully graced the sky.

Where they retreat to, I do not know,
nor do I need to.

Yet I know for sure, as the next evening
approaches, I will once again be greeted
by another humble cast.

Perhaps this cast will lead me
to a standing ovation.

Happiness

I merely need a vehicle to express myself.

The Greats

Before you lies a stage, its curtains drawn.

Bit by bit, the curtains open and magically
before you, a whole other world appears.

A light shines down and your attention
is drawn to center stage.

Two silhouettes emerge, representing all
those who have proceeded them.

Their task is not a simple one;
the shoes, not easily filled.

Their quest is to revive those who now
only live on in our memories.

The characters are numerous but the
understudies do not falter for many hours
have been spent learning the secrets
of those now gone.

They have not replaced 'The Greats',
nor will they ever.

They are merely showing their gratitude
to those who have led the way.

Peace, Joy and Beauty

There are days when peace is easy to come by.

There are days when being thankful for the small
things will make your day more joyous.

There are days when appreciating the beauty in
everything will make you smile more.

If today is not one of peace, joy and beauty,
I challenge you to look around your
surroundings or the deepest realms of
your imagination and create that
magical place for yourself.

Then wrap your arms around it so tightly,
that it becomes ingrained in your mind
for easy access anytime you need it.

Make peace, joy and beauty your closest friends
and know they will be there for you
anytime you need them.

For when you are open to them,
they will never fail you.

Dirt Roads

I drove from paved roads to dirt roads
that lead to…? Where, I was not sure.

With windows down, the fresh breeze of the
country air drifted from side to side
as dust settled throughout my vehicle.

I pulled over whenever my spirit caught wind
of a babbling brook or abandoned building.

I thought, 'how sad these roads are barren,
as they are both picturesque and freeing'.

A world of magic exists within these curving
roads and rolling hills, a world no paved road
will ever endow.

Injustice

Enjoy if you wish,

The Writers Mind

I have the capacity to write but today,
the words fail to flow from pen to paper.

Others my look at the blank page
as a clean canvas, and create
meaningful thoughts with ease.

But tonight, for me, my writers mind is blank.

There is no concentration as my mind
has left me dangling.

As phrases elude me, I start to feel the walls
entrap me like a prisoner in a jail cell;
I am unable to break free.

I have broken no law, yet a force greater than I,
has deprived me of my rightful gift and
left me barren of all thought.

One way or another, I must find a way to fill
this painful emptiness or spend the last hours
of this day, with eyes gazing upon brilliant
white paper teeming with invisible words.

You Decide

There are too many walls that separate us.

Too many windows to see through.

Mismatched colours which have no meaning.

Footprints lead the way, some egotistical and chauvinistic while others are kind and giving.

A ghostlike reflection filters through the room, while journals flash back in time.

Reflective glass shows all I am or may be, while another dream is shattered.

Leaving me alone with a parade of shapes and colours, none of them predefined.

Volcano Anger

An anger arises out of me, like molten lava
erupting out of a volcano.

I work to keep it in check but it spills forth,
slow at first and then gains speed.

I do not understand why I can't control it, but
more importantly why the anger is so powerful.

I scream at everyone in my mind.

My body chills as I try to figure out
this puzzle of anger.

No luck!

I pray I have the strength to hold it together
for breaking down serves no purpose.

Conceivably I am not the only one to feel this
way but in this moment at this time, it is only me
I can consciously care about.

Truth

While attempting to make sense of my life,
I keep thinking about our situation and I am
being lead in too many different directions.

I then wonder, 'is there a point to any of this'?

Our world has become a bizarre place,
one I do not understand.

Perhaps I never will.

From what I have observed, you don't have a
clue, and it is a sad state of affairs when I can
see what stands in front of you and yet you
remain blind to the obvious.

There is a chance that you are choosing not to
face the truth or the error of your ways… but oh,
how I wish you would, for I'm tired of hurting
and dealing with this pain.

And therefore, I must withhold my sympathy
and leave you to your journey for one of us
must be strong.

And from all that I have seen that
one of us is me.

Pain

A vision has left me saddened and yet no matter
how hard I try, I cannot erase the image and the
anguish from my heart; a vision that forces me to
remember that which I would rather forget.

A face devoid of happiness, eyes no longer see
and a tail no longer wags.

A soul has been broken and days of
carefree living, gone.

I watch from a distance, feeling its pain.

Then unwillingly, I am forced to
take another look.

With luck, his days are numbered and
the pain will soon subside.

I wish him a safe journey to his final destination,
where unlimited peace awaits,
for he has suffered enough.

Tears slide down my face as
my heart continues to ache.

Never will I forget the tormented expression or
forgive those who provoked it in the first place.

Love

understand if you can,
but regardless,

Existence

The night air sends shivers through my body
as I sit on the cold concrete porch.

Street lamps illuminate the darkened streets and
in the distance, I hear the sound of racing cars.

My mind is blank except for thoughts of you.

As I stare endlessly into the night, I pray for
daybreak, so I may once again hear your
comforting voice, if only for a moment.

For now, my thoughts of you will have to suffice.

Perhaps one day, it won't just be the sound of
your voice that holds me close and keeps me safe,
it will also be the warmth of your body as you
entangle me in your arms.

The Dream

I fall fast asleep as the night envelopes me
like a cloak.

I am rendered helpless as you enter my dreams.

The strength of your arms, the caress
of your hands and sweet kisses all over
my body cause me to lose control.

My breathing increases as our passion intensifies,
and only you can extinguish the fire which
comes from the feelings of love that we share.

My dream may not last, but I know
your love for me will live on forever.

ForEver

A young woman sits at her desk with pen and
blank paper before her.

She is anxious to find the right words to
let her father know how important his presence
is in her life but nothing is forthcoming.

She is distracted by classical music playing
softly in the background, as she shifts her
gaze around the room.

Neither the pictures which adorn the walls or the
twenty-eight years of memories are enough to
provide the needed inspiration.

The world outside continues to revolve,
as it is not able to wait for the woman
hidden behind stone walls.

She wonders the words needed to send
their meaning and if they will be understood.

She needs her father to know she loves him
and all she has learned through their
many years together.

His spirit and encouragement
have been invaluable.

She realizes he will not live forever, yet no matter
where his is, his love for her will prevail.

ForEver *(continued)*

Her memories of years gone by continue to fade
but not the love that got them this far.

Her message to her dear father, is simple,
'Nothing will ever change the love I feel for you,
for I am yours forevermore'.

Love Me

They make you believe it's possible.

The novels, the movies, the papers.

Some say it lasts forever and never dies.

It comes in all shapes and styles.

It's there to give and there to take.

I have read about it, I have seen it on TV and
I believe it, but have I really felt it?

We search the earth and sometimes beyond
looking for this mysterious feeling.

Highly overrated, one person said.

Another said nothing at all.

It's not always said and it's not always shared.

It's simply there in black and white.

There's more to love than saying it,
it's in what you do as well.

It's a skill I've never mastered but when it comes
right down to it, love was all I ever wanted.

A Love so Pure

When I look into your eyes, I see love.

So I shall take this moment and all others and
treasure them deep within my heart.

Your presence in my life has brought me
endless joy and I can't imagine being
with another living soul.

I am eternally blessed for each special moment
we share, not only today but every day until
our last breaths are taken from within.

A Christmas Memory

A child of years gone by, reflects on the
memories so bright that even as she ages
year by year, they never fade.

She remembers twinkling lights, the smell of
burning wood and the taste of warmed cider.

She remembers the ornaments as if
they were hung only yesterday.

She remembers the love and care that went
into decorating the magical tree.

Beneath its branches, in radiant greens,
reds and gold the presents shone.

The child eagerly rehearsed the placement of
gifts, knowing exactly those meant for her.

She awoke as Christmas morning neared
but dawn had not yet broken through
the blackness of the sky.

She climbed carefully from the warmth of her
bed and ventured to the top of the stairs.

There her eyes quickly widened, for the lights
of the tree brought to life the excitement
the child held deep within, for soon it
would be Christmas morning.

Santa had come, the child could feel
the warmth of his presence.

A Christmas Memory (continued)

He had brought not only gifts, but love as well.

A love she felt so freely.

As quietly as she had ventured from her room, she returned and snuggled once again within the sheets that kept her warm throughout the chilly winter nights.

The warmth quickly brought rest to the weary girl but not before she whispered, 'I love you Santa'.

The light in the child's mind quickly dims, but the memory, all these years later, lives on.

Happy Anniversary

Where we are today.

Life is a journey which takes us through many different experiences.

Some good and some bad, it is what we make of those experiences that is important.

We have now shared 10 years of ups and downs and roundabouts.

One could say we work hard at driving each other crazy and one could say we go out of our way to be there for each other.

It is always when I least expect it that you go out of your way for me.

It is the little things that I love the most.

They bring me the greatest joy and show me how true your love is for me.

I may not be the best at showing my love and gratitude, and I have my days, but know this: I do love you and even though you don't always believe me, I'm lucky to have you in my life because when I need you, you're there.

And that is what really counts.

Pain

all that concerns me is that you
don't judge me for the honesty
I present to myself.

Freed o m
lives within the
CREATIVE walls
of my
Emerging Spirit

Object of Whose Desire?

Did you see me pass in the moonlight?

Did you ever see the glistening tear drops on my
cheeks as we shared moments of heated passion?

My breath, always ragged as we came
together as one but my expectations of
our relationship, haunt me constantly.

Was our relationship about us as a couple or
simply about what you needed and wanted?

Was I ever any more than just an object to you?

My life has been filled with rejections
regardless of how hard I have tried.

I understand no one, least of all myself during
the darkest moments of my life.

I console myself, with random memories
of happier times.

How do you remember me?

Do you smile and think happy thoughts OR
do you think back to the first time when
your hope was I would simply disappear?

Once an object, always an object but up until
the point where you threw me away,
I continued to love you, no matter what.

Condition X

We, like the petals of a flower, reach towards the
noon day sun for its warmth and yet, not all days
are filled with the sun's nourishing rays.

There are days, both chilling and dark,
from which we cannot hide.

Some days our souls are bared, looking for
protection, but none is forthcoming.

The cold unforgiving darkness does not
understand our plight, nor does it try.

Why does the darkness mock us,
as it drains our energy?

Why does it not realize the support we need?

And more importantly, why do we continue
to open ourselves up, when in reality, unlike
the fragile flower, we have a choice between
pure light and never ending darkness.

The Hurt Factor

It slips from my mind on occasion.

It comes and goes, like night and day.

It gnaws away at my soul while sleep is lost and
many hours are wasted.

The pain is immense and the scars go deep.

Moods evolve, change and darken producing
an aura as dark as coal.

It seethes and broods as it builds
moment to moment and day to day.

It's experienced, it's realized and it
contaminates all that it comes in contact with.

But at its most powerful,
it destroys many in its wake.

A Stranger's Evil

The eyes of a stranger delve deep into your soul.

Days becomes weeks and the attraction grows,
into something neither of us imagined.

Your heart goes one way while
your mind goes another.

They battle each other in an attempt to control.

You mind is aware of the commitments bound.

While your heart only thinks of the prize to be
won, the power of another is engulfing you
from all sides.

Their magic immense, and your desire too great.

Their spell must be broken, your heart set free.

To continue this cycle will destroy us all.

Shed yourself of this demon,
give your mind back control.

A Broken Heart

I saw an image of you today, another with
the same sleek black and mahogany fur,
the stubby tail and powerful build.

It reminded me of our time together.

How we played for hours, took long walks and
lay together late at night.

You were carefree and loving,
you gave all you had.

In return, all you asked for was a home full of
love where you could live out the rest of your life.

Circumstances within, but outside my control,
had me letting you go too soon, and now your
memory haunts me, sometimes for days on end.

Another has since come into my life but the love
I had for you will never be replaced.

That sacred place within my heart,
is yours forevermore.

Cobblestone

Through the cobblestone streets of England,
I did wander.

The day was cold, dark and rainy.

I could feel the warmth of my rich red blood as
it pumped through my body, even though the
dampness would have sent a chill through most.

My mind chose to focus on nothing in particular.

A heavy heart was mine to bear
on this dreary day.

A feeling of sadness overwhelmed me, the reason
as unclear as the day itself.

Those passing by me were like ghosts,
shadows easily missed, like feelings
I have often chosen to ignore.

In moments like these I try to be still,
not because I can but, simply, because I must.

Love Destroyed

I look at my life sometimes and wonder where
I'm going, for as life passes me by,
I remain stalled.

I wanted to understand how I fit into the picture
of life you created for us, yet each time I looked
at it, I became increasingly confused by it.

Your betrayal devastated me, but you
couldn't see past yourself as my pain was
cruelly brushed aside.

I wonder, did you ever CARE,
did you ever LOVE me?

I feared you didn't but hoped
foolishly that you did.

My mistake.

I gave until I could give no more.

My pain so great, my expectations destroyed.

You moved on, I stopped dead in my tracks.

My life, I have tried to rebuild it,
but the mortar won't hold.

I loved you more than you know.

You hurt me more than you know.

In my quest for love, I asked the wrong person.

Love Destroyed (continued)

My pain is great and so are my regrets.

Thanks for all you didn't do.

You got your wish for love, I did not.

I taught you the meaning of love, you taught me
the meaning of rejection.

You never deserved me, and perhaps one day you
will realize your loss.

No one could love you more but the perfection
you sought, I could not learn.

I did more than expected,
but it was never enough.

I deserved the world and so much more.

Thanks for nothing because NOTHING was all
you gave me, and shame on me for accepting.

Glitter without Happiness

The beautiful objects that glitter,
how do they make you feel?

As I look around, I wonder why it has been
so important to me to own things that
I can't take with me when I die.

Some days these material objects
don't even make me happy.

I compare myself to others whose tastes are
so much simpler and see they are content.

I'm not sure I have ever been content and
I'm not sure I would even recognize it if I were.

Now, that's sad.

The Dot

It was a dot surrounded by inches and inches of
plain beige paint that reached floor to ceiling.

It was a dot in the middle of an
otherwise vacant wall.

It stood alone and frightened on
that great big wall.

Then, a fresh coat of paint covered the dot.

Now hidden, it's safe, its uniqueness gone.

A distant memory - forgotten, not missed.

I'm like that dot; covered beneath
layers of misguided beliefs and thoughts.

And like the dot, I am not missed at all.

Consider This

Some ponder the philosophy that
'time heals all wounds'.

Yet, is it true?

When tragedy strikes, we are not
all programmed to easily forget.

For some, our painful memories live on
indefinitely while our happy moments
fade too quickly.

We may ask ourselves if that which we perceive
is real or imaginary and then we struggle to
understand why the memories that hurt
so much persist as long as they do.

Is guilt a factor here?

Is all that is unfortunate a result of our
own doing and pain our penance?

Happy, carefree moments elude me.

The images of mistakes I've made remain
embedded in my mind.

I do not believe one should struggle to
remember the good times – they should
always remain vivid.

So how does one encourage the best to remain?

If one could succeed in finding this answer, it
would be a blessing for all.

Time

*For unlike some,
I play with words,
not people.*

The
Squelch Artistic

Why Being

The Who
Most In
Sees
Colourful World
Of Ways? The

Fantasy

In the middle of a room, a lone poet stands.

Candles are lit to provide the
necessary light needed to write a poem.

Music in the background provides inspiration,
as does the soft falling snow outside
the room's only window.

A glass of wine soothes the soul as
the poet's creative juices flow.

A castle-like building can be seen
across the street.

It takes the poet back to a time of kings, queens,
fancy balls, flowing gowns, food and laughter.

As Christmas nears the poet is
reminded of its magical powers.

A time of fantasy, when anything is possible.

Where we choose to live in a world of reality
364 days of the year, isn't it important that at
least one day of the year be fantasy bound?

Truth within the Picture

Determined concentration allows you
to discover one's innermost secrets.

A painted picture, under close scrutiny,
may render one to understand
the thoughts and feelings of another.

The vibrant or muted colours may elude to the
temperament, while the scenery to the story.

An innocent child and playful dog personify
our innocence, while geometric shapes
may reflect the changes that occur over time.

A spectrum of colour may represent our
many sides, stretching from absolute beauty
to wicked darkness.

Our shadows on the wall reflect who we are and
perhaps we are able to deceive those around us
but we cannot deceive ourselves.

Our reflection is a reminder of who we are,
but the child within is a reminder of who
we would rather be.

When

The notebook lay on the couch, open to the
last page, where I had written about you.

We truly have no understanding
of the time we have on earth.

We have no control over when the end will come.

I heard love and excitement in your voice and
although your eyes spoke volumes,
I never had any idea how your heart felt.

Your memory will live with me forever.

When my end comes, may I never forget
the joy you brought into my life.

Random Emotions

I picked up a notebook, its price unknown to me.

Did I need it? No.

It was simply bought out of want.

A poor reason by some peoples standards.

To assuage myself of guilt, I filled the pages
with emotions that overtook me.

And as I wrote, I thought of my fathers.

Both gone and yet there are moments
when their spirits surround me.

Though my loss was great, I now understand
grief and respect but what scares me most
is losing my mother.

That moment will be sheer hell
for some things in life, one just knows.

Your Wilderness

You wake in the morning, dress and head out the door to a place you no longer want to go.

You spend hours getting nowhere, only to go back the next day.

There are others in the world who struggle as you do and still others who love what they do, day in and day out.

When you leave at the end of the day, you wish to cast it all aside…yet there are days when your job follows you home. This creates great sadness.

You no longer just wish for some other job, you wish for the job you were truly meant to have.

A job where your spirit soars and time becomes your best friend.

The time has come for us to reach beyond the stone walls of our old beliefs and instead wrap our arms around the outer walls of the wilderness where our heart sings every day.

Realization

It is virtually impossible to be discovered
when locked away by your own admission.

The door to your freedom is as simple
as turning a handle.

You need no instructions and there are no tips
or tricks, just a door, and any locks you perceive,
may only exist in your imagination and
not on the door itself.

As you bide your time waiting for the
world to find you, you curse the injustice:
'how can they be so blind…don't they
already know my brilliance?'

The time has come for you to open your eyes and
the door to your freedom: to impart all you have
to the masses. Once this simple step is fulfilled,
the rest of your life will fall into place.

Timeless Window

If you look outside the window,
you will see the face of time.

Be it spring, summer, fall, winter, day or night.

It will show you all that has been and perhaps
what is to come, if you are willing to open up,
to your endless possibilities.

The memories of your past, have wrapped
around your mind as your soul reaches for
the future and that which you aspire to;
whether that be moments of peace and
tranquility or moments of high energy
doing what you were called here to do.

So let the window be your guide in time and
trust it will lead you in your quest.

For your moment of knowing will take you
to places you never imagined.

A Moment of Peace

For a moment, calmness settled over my body.

My mind did not think as I
boiled water for my tea.

The presence of my life did not bother me.

Patiently, I waited for the water to boil.

I thought of nothing sad, nothing troubling and
nothing which would anger me.

I simply stood, waited, and when the water was
ready, I poured it into a well-worn china tea cup.

As I took a spoon from a kitchen drawer,
I took note of the flashing light on the answering
machine but made no motion to address it.

I finished preparing my tea, then headed to
the seclusion of my creative studio in
another part of the house.

For a moment, life was calm.

For a moment, life was as I had always
envisioned it would be.

Simply for a moment.

My Vehicle

It has never been my expectation that
everyone would understand my thoughts.

For you see, the sky is not always clear and
bright in my world, and that is okay with me.

My love is writing, and no matter what I write,
I don't need your approval.

I merely need a vehicle to express myself.

Enjoy if you wish, understand if you can, but
regardless, all that concerns me is that you don't
judge me for the honesty I present to myself.

For unlike some, I play with words, not people.

About the Author

Natalie Merritt-Broderick has been writing since the age of thirteen. Writing non-fiction has allowed her to re-evaluate her life, find solutions and speak her truth, all from a place of passion. While writing fiction has allowed her to display her vivid imagination.

Natalie has published a number of articles and shared her experiences on her website. Through her writing, creative art and speaking, she wants to inspire others to fulfill their dreams and realize how important it is to share their creative gifts with others, each and every day.

Natalie will continue to write and speak about life and what is truly important to her as long as paper and pen exist in her world. Her writing has allowed her to be who she is meant to be and she graciously thanks the Universe for giving her the ability to write and speak from the heart, a place she spends the majority of her time.

22351394R00048

Made in the USA
Columbia, SC
31 July 2018